The Wayland Library of Science and Technology

MANUFACTURING INDUSTRY

ROBIN KERROD

The Wayland Library of Science and Technology

The Nature of Matter
The Universal Forces
Stars and Galaxies
The Solar System
The Changing Landscape
Air and Oceans
Origins of Life
The Science of Life
Plants and Animals
Animal Behaviour
The Human Machine
Health and Medicine

The Environment
Feeding the World
Raw Materials
Manufacturing Industry
Energy Sources
The Power Generators
Transport
Space Travel
Communications
The Computer Age
Scientific Instruments
Towards Tomorrow

Advisory Series Editor
Robin Kerrod

Consultant
Dr. J. Beynon

Editor: Caroline Sheldrick
Design: Cooper-Wilson
Picture Research: Alison Renney
Production: Steve Elliott
Art Director: John Ridgeway
Project Director: Lawrence Clarke

First published in 1990 by
Wayland (Publishers) Ltd
61 Western Road, Hove
East Sussex BN3 1JD, England

 AN EQUINOX BOOK

Planned and produced by:
Equinox (Oxford) Limited
Musterlin House, Jordan Hill Road,
Oxford OX2 8DP

Copyright © Equinox (Oxford) Ltd 1990

British Library Cataloguing in Publication Data
Kerrod, Robin
    Manufacturing industry.
    1. Manufacturing industries
    I. Title
    670.427

ISBN 0-7502-0022-7

Media conversion and typesetting by Peter
MacDonald, Una Macnamara and Vanessa Hersey
Origination by Hong Kong Reprohouse Co Ltd
Printed in Italy by Rotolito Lombarda
S.p.A., Milan
Bound in France by AGM

Front cover: A fleet of Japanese cars being
exported.
Back cover: A diagram showing part of the
process of distillation of malt whisky.

Contents

Introduction

The word manufacturing literally means "making by hand". But the vast majority of the products we use, from ball-bearings and bottles to carpets and cars, are manufactured by machines in factories.

Machines hold the key to modern manufacturing, particularly machines controlled by computers. Computers are changing our industries, pattern of employment and way of life very rapidly. These changes may be as great as those that occurred during the Industrial Revolution of the 1700s.

This volume outlines how major branches of the manufacturing industry transform materials into finished products. It covers metalworking techniques, such as forging and welding; chemical technologies, such as acid and plastics manufacture; food processing and synthesizing drugs; papermaking, spinning and weaving, and production of the miracle of the age, the silicon chip.

◄ Imported cars from Japan. Advances in steelmaking have made cars cheap enough for many to own them. The car-making industry pioneered the assembly-line method of industrial production.

Production

Spot facts

- *The introduction of the Bessemer steelmaking process in 1856 reduced the cost of steel by more than 90 per cent, to about £3 a ton.*

- *The introduction of automation in some heavy industries, such as steelmaking, has reduced the workforce by up to 90 per cent.*

- *The introduction of computers and word processors in business, which was supposed to bring about the "paperless office", has in fact led to a marked increase in world paper consumption.*

▶ An operator at the control console of an automated steel-rolling mill. In the mill a red-hot slab of steel passes at ever-increasing speed between sets of heavy rollers. The control computer automatically sets the gap between each set of rollers according to the temperature and thickness of the steel coming from the previous set of rollers.

Most of our goods are made or processed in factories by machines. Machines were first introduced on a wide scale during the Industrial Revolution, which began in Britain in the early 1700s and spread gradually to the rest of the world. It did more than change industry. It also changed people's lives. People flocked from the land into towns to work in factories. What had been a rural society started to become an industrial one.

The use of machines in factories and the careful organization of labour are still the key factors in manufacturing today. They allow the efficient mass-production of goods at low cost.

The Industrial Revolution

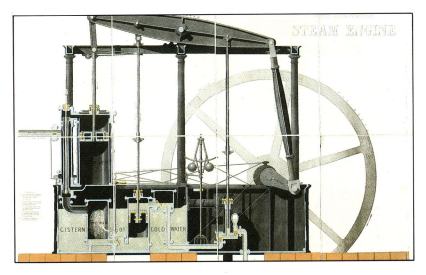

◀ James Watt's double-acting steam engine of the 1780s, the machine that powered the Industrial Revolution. Steam was introduced to each side of the piston in turn, making each piston stroke (movement) a power stroke. With its separate condenser, it was four times more powerful than Thomas Newcomen's engine of the early 1700s.

▼ Four milestones in the development of industry. The spinning jenny helped transform textile-making into an industry. The screw-cutting lathe was one of the first precision machine tools. The *Rocket* locomotive ushered in a revolution in transport; the Bessemer process, a revolution in steelmaking.

Perhaps surprisingly, the Industrial Revolution began in textile-making. This ancient craft was transformed from a domestic activity into an industry by a series of inventions in spinning and weaving. In 1733 John Kay invented a mechanical shuttle, which greatly speeded up weaving. This created an increased demand for spun yarn. And so in turn came James Hargreaves, with the spinning jenny (1767); Richard Arkwright, with the water frame (1769); and Samuel Crompton, with the spinning mule (1779); with machines to spin yarn faster.

Now the looms could not cope with the extra yarn, and so Edmund Cartwright built a steam-powered loom (1785) to speed weaving. With speedier spinning and weaving, the cotton-growers in the United States could no longer supply cotton fast enough. But in 1792 an American, Eli Whitney, speeded up the slowest part of cotton production: separating the fibres from the seeds. His cotton gin could separate the fibres 50 times faster than by hand.

The application of steam power to industry began first in coalmining in the early 1700s. First Thomas Savery and then Thomas Newcomen devised steam-pumping machines. But it took the genius of James Watt to convert the steam engine into a reliable and compact power source. The success of Watt's engine in turn depended on John Wilkinson's invention (1775) of a machine for boring the engine cylinder accurately. And so it went on, with each invention playing its part in a revolution that has continued to the present day.

Milestones in the Industrial Revolution

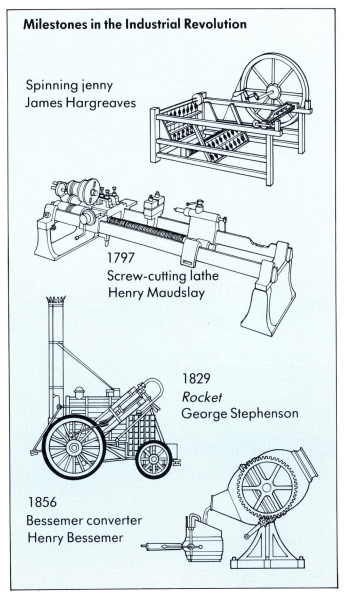

Spinning jenny
James Hargreaves

1797
Screw-cutting lathe
Henry Maudslay

1829
Rocket
George Stephenson

1856
Bessemer converter
Henry Bessemer

The factory

▶ Richard Arkwright invented this roller-spinning machine in 1769. On the machine a loose "rope" of fibres was drawn out into fine yarn by sets of rotating rollers. Then the yarn was twisted by a rotating "flyer" as it was wound on to a bobbin. The machine was driven by a moving belt from a waterwheel and was known as a water frame.

Richard Arkwright invented the water frame spinning machine, but he has a greater claim to fame. In 1771 he installed a large number of water frames in a building at Cromford, in Derbyshire. He employed people to operate them, so pioneering the factory system.

Cloth is an example of a product that is made directly from raw materials. Many other goods are produced by assembling, or putting together, sets of ready-made components that are nearly identical. This method was pioneered in the late 1700s by Eli Whitney.

In 1798 Whitney contracted to produce 10,000 muskets for the army in two years. This was a tall order because even a highly skilled gunsmith could make only a few guns in a year. He would make all the parts himself and tailor

them to fit together. Each musket was slightly different. Whitney tackled the problem another way. First he designed machines that could turn out near-identical parts each time. He employed skilled engineers for this part of the operation. Then he employed unskilled people to assemble the muskets from sets of parts. In this venture Whitney established another manufacturing principle: the use of precision machine tools to create near-identical, or interchangeable parts, which can then be put together by semiskilled labour.

The American car-maker Henry Ford established another manufacturing principle in 1913. That year he introduced the moving assembly line into his factory making the famous "Model T" Ford. In this method of assembly, workers were positioned at some 50 points next to a track, along which moved the car frame. As the frame moved past, each worker would attach a part to it until, at the end of the line, the car was complete. Since each worker had only to perform one task, it could be done very quickly indeed.

The latest chapter in the factory story features computers. Machines, machine tools and even whole production networks are being brought under computer control. This leads to automation, a system in which machines regulate themselves. Modern factories incorporate some or all of these features: machines, precision machine tools, interchangeable parts, moving assembly lines, and automatic computer control.

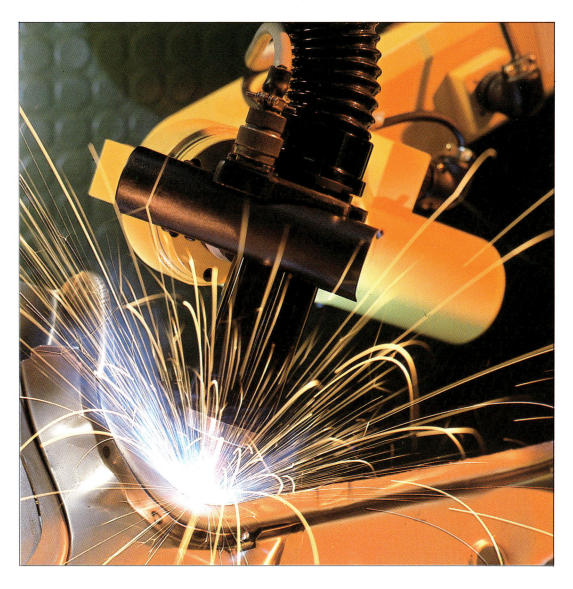

◄ The production line in an automated factory making Macintosh computers. No human workers are to be seen. The few workers there are in the factory are present to oversee operations. Computer-manufacture hinges on the production of silicon chips and electronic circuits, which can be designed and checked only by other computers.

► A robot welder at work. Robot welding machines are now common in manufacturing. They work accurately and are unaffected by heat, glare and fumes. A camera sends pictures of the exact position of the workpiece to the robot, which adjusts its arm in order to make the weld in the correct position.

Organization

The production of goods by machines in a factory is the visible aspect of manufacturing. But there are many other aspects, including design, sales, market research, finance and labour relations. For example, the products being made must be of the right design and sell at the right price. Otherwise, nobody will buy them. Market research will often need to be carried out to find out from potential customers what are the right goods and the right price. Enough goods must be sold to pay for the cost of setting up production, paying for raw materials, paying the workforce, and so on. The workers must be paid a reasonable wage for what they do and be given reasonable working conditions. Otherwise, they will become discontented, disputes will break out, and production will be lost.

For a manufacturing operation to work

▶ Picking grapes for winemaking in the Loire region of France. Many of the small French wine-producers have formed cooperatives. These are loose companies in which members share winemaking equipment and marketing facilities, yet still remain largely independent.

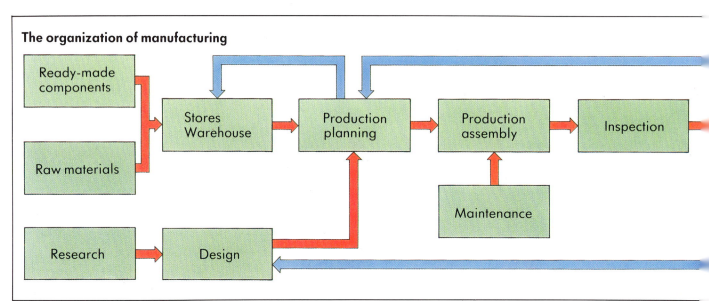

The organization of manufacturing

Ready-made components · Raw materials → Stores Warehouse → Production planning → Production assembly → Inspection

Maintenance → Production assembly

Research → Design

successfully, it must be well-organized in every aspect. The kind of organization needed varies widely according to the size and nature of the operation. In a small company, which employs only a handful of people, the owner takes responsibility for everything, from design to marketing and employee relations.

The management

In a large company, however, reponsibilities are shared by a team of managers. Each is responsible for the operation and organization of a department, which deals with one aspect of the manufacturing operation, such as production, sales and marketing. The managers have staff under them, who carry out their instructions. In turn the managers carry out policies laid down by a board of directors.

In a large company, the directors may be answerable to shareholders. These are people who have invested money in the company by buying shares. Their money provides working capital for the company, enabling it to develop new processes and new products in order to increase sales and make extra profit. The company pays the shareholders a dividend, or percentage of any profit they make.

Producing the goods

The initial idea for a new product may come from a variety of sources. For example, the sales team may spot a gap in the market. Or company scientists may make a brilliant discovery. The idea is taken up by the design and research departments, which look at the possible new product from every viewpoint. For example, they may experiment with different kinds of materials to find the one most suitable; and they will investigate methods of production. They may build mock-ups, or full-size models, of the product, and maybe one or more prototypes, or examples of the finished product.

If the new project is given the go-ahead, production planners draw up detailed plans for manufacturing. They work out what raw materials, tools, machines and workers are required to produce the goods in the numbers required. And they draw up schedules and flowcharts to ensure that the right materials, tools, machines and workers are always in the right place at the right time in the process.

The manufacturing process will involve the production of components from raw materials, or the assembly of components into a finished product, or both. Machining operations by machine tools will often be involved. After manufacture, the goods will be inspected and periodically tested. Any substandard ones will be rejected. This is called quality control. The goods are finally packaged ready for distribution to retailers or wholesalers. Retailers sell the goods to the public; wholesalers sell to retailers. Sometimes the goods may be sold directly to customers by the sales team.

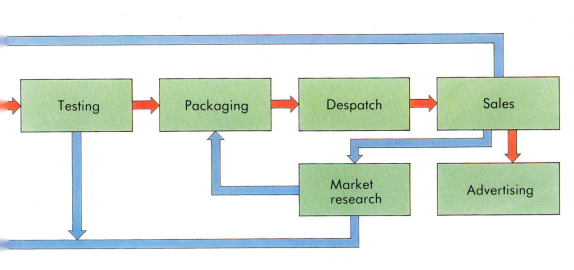

Important stages in the manufacturing process, from the arrival of raw materials and components to the distribution and sale of the manufactured product. As can be seen, actual production is only part of the set-up. Many of the stages are linked because there is a feedback of information from one to the other.

Working with metals

Most of the metals we use are produced by smelting ores at high temperatures in furnaces. They leave the furnace in a molten state. They then have to be processed into finished products. The shaping process selected depends on the metal concerned and what it is to be used for. A metal may be shaped when it is molten, when red-hot or when cold. It may be moulded, rolled, hammered, squeezed or welded. Afterwards it may be turned, ground, drilled or milled to very precise dimensions by machine tools. Precision machining holds the key to most manufacturing processes.

► White-hot steel pours into a travelling ladle from an electric-arc furnace. Next it will be cast into moulds, where it will solidify into ingots. These will then go to other machines for final shaping.

Casting

The technique of shaping metals by casting has been practised for at least 6,000 years. Casting is a process in which molten metal is poured into shaped moulds and allowed to cool. As it cools, it sets, or becomes solid, and takes the shape of the mould. Copper and bronze were the first metals shaped by casting because they could be melted in the early furnaces. Bronze is still widely used for casting, to make such things as statues and ships' propellers. The most common casting metal, however, is iron. Machinery bodies such as engine blocks are cast in iron, because cast iron is hard and rigid.

Sand casting

Casting takes place in a foundry. The most common method is sand casting. A model of the object to be made is placed in a box and a moist sand and clay mixture is packed tightly around it. A cavity of the required shape remains when the model is removed. Usually the mould is made in two halves to allow the model to be removed. Two holes are made in the top of the mould. The metal is poured in through one (called the runner), while the other (the riser) allows the air to escape from inside. The mould is broken up to release the casting when cool.

In a variation of this process, the model is made in wax. After the mould has been made, it is heated and the wax is poured out. Molten metal is then poured in. This method is called investment casting or the lost-wax (*cire perdue*) process. It is often used by artists, and to make precision castings for engines.

Diecasting

This is a method of casting that takes place in a metal mould, or die, which can be used over and over again. It is sometimes called permanent-mould casting. In gravity diecasting, molten metal is poured into a mould. It is suitable for producing simple shapes such as pipes.

More intricate shapes can be produced by injecting molten metal into a water-cooled mould under pressure. This method is widely used to make parts for machines and appliances. Alloys containing zinc, tin, aluminium and magnesium are favoured because they have a low melting point. Pressure diecasting is very suitable for mass-production.

▲ Workers handling a still red-hot casting of a railway wagon wheel, which has just been removed from its mould. It is cast in steel.

Sand casting

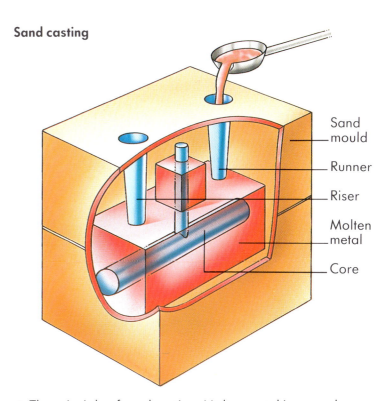

Sand mould

Runner

Riser

Molten metal

Core

▲ The principle of sand casting. Molten metal is poured into a hollow mould, which has the shape of the object to be made. To produce a hollow object, a core must be included. The metal is poured into the mould until it fills both the runner and the riser.

Rolling

Rolling is a process in which metal is passed between heavy rotating rollers, rather like clothes through an old-fashioned mangle. In a rolling mill the metal is passed through a succession of rollers, each pair being slightly closer together than those before. In this way the metal is squeezed thinner and thinner. Mostly, metal is rolled when it is red-hot. In this state it can "flow" more easily.

Much of the metal produced in furnaces is first cast into ingots. Usually these are then reduced to a more convenient size by rolling. The metal emerges as a flat slab, which may then go for shaping by another method, such as forging. Or it may be rolled further, for example, in a continuous strip mill. This produces coils of thin sheet, or strip. The slab goes slowly into the first set of rollers, but comes from the last set travelling at a speed of up to 100 km/h. The hot-rolled strip is then usually rolled again when cold. Cold rolling improves the surface finish and increases the hardness.

▲ Steel strip coming off a cold-rolling mill. During cold rolling the metal becomes brittle, which could cause it to crack in use. It therefore undergoes a heat treatment called annealing to bring it back to a reasonable condition. It is first heated and then it is allowed to cool slowly.

◄ High above the city streets, workers piece together a frame of iron girders that will support a new tower block. The girders are shaped with a typical H cross-section in rolling mills, using rollers with grooves cut in them.

Forging and pressing

Forging shapes metal by hammering. It is the oldest shaping method. In early times metals were forged by hand in much the same way that a traditional blacksmith does today. But in industry today forging is done by machine.

In a drop forge, the hammering action is produced by a falling hammer, or ram. The ram is raised again by air or steam pressure. Air or steam pressure may also be used to help accelerate the ram downwards to deliver an even more powerful blow. The ram shapes the metal by forcing it into a mould, or die.

Usually the ram carries the upper part of the die, while the lower part is mounted on the forge bed. The metal blank, usually hot, is placed on the lower die, and the ram is released. The metal is forced into shape as the two halves of the die come together. Stamping is a kind of small-scale drop-forging process used to make coins and medals.

On a forging press metal is forced into shape, not by a hammer blow, but by a gradual squeezing action. The press works by hydraulic (liquid) pressure. Some presses can exert a force of up to 50,000 tonnes. They are used, for example, to shape massive red-hot steel ingots. Smaller hydraulic presses are used to shape car body panels from cold steel sheet.

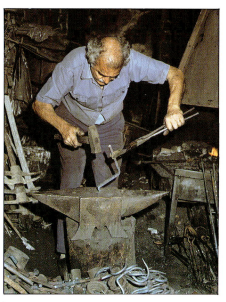

▲ A blacksmith practises the traditional craft of forging. A strip of metal is heated up in the forge fire, and then hammered into shape on an anvil. Metal is cooled by plunging it into cold water.

◀ Forging the rotor shaft of a turbine on a massive forging press. The shaft is beginning to take shape. It started off as an ingot casting, which was reheated until it was red hot. Then it was placed on the press and slowly squeezed into shape under a pressure of thousands of tonnes exerted by the hydraulic ram. Later, it will be machined on a lathe to bring it to the dimensions required in a rotor shaft.

Joining metals

Riveting

Many metal objects are so large or so complicated that they cannot be produced in one piece, but must be built up little by little. A ship's hull is an example. Until about the middle of the century, most hulls were built of steel plates joined together by rivets. A rivet is a metal plug with a rounded head at one end.

In riveting, holes are drilled in overlapping plates. Rivets are inserted through them and hammered to form a second head. The metal plates are then sandwiched tightly together. Riveting is no longer much used for producing ships' hulls, although it is still widely used elsewhere in shipbuilding. It is also used in aircraft construction for building the airframe and the outer "skin" of the fuselage and wings.

Welding

Most ships' hulls these days are constructed of steel plates that are welded together. The plates are joined edge to edge, with no overlap, which saves weight and materials.

In welding, the edges of the metal pieces to be joined are brought into contact and heated until they begin to melt and merge, or fuse together.

▶ A welder joins together two lengths of pipeline for the North Sea oilfields. The method is electric welding, using a special circular electrode. The welder wears thick protective clothing and a head mask as protection against the shower of sparks and glare which the welding process generates.

▼ These are the two main methods of producing a strong joint between pieces of metal. In riveting, headed rivets clamp overlapping metal plates together. In welding, joints are produced when touching pieces of metal melt and fuse together. Welded joints can be of different types, which include butt, lap, fillet and spot welds.

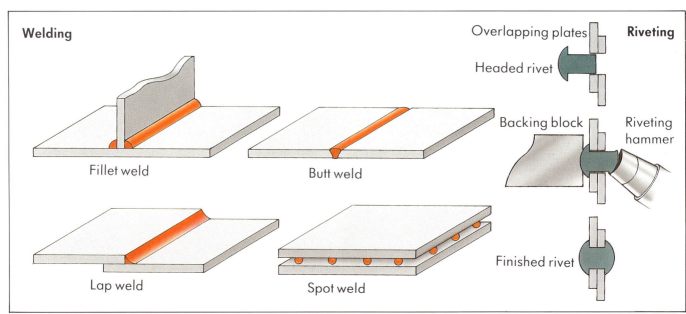

Welding

Fillet weld

Butt weld

Lap weld

Spot weld

Overlapping plates — **Riveting**

Headed rivet

Backing block

Riveting hammer

Finished rivet

Extra molten metal is often added from a so-called filler rod. When the metal in the joint cools, it forms a continuous structure linking the two pieces. The result is a strong joint.

There are three main methods of welding – gas, arc and resistance welding. In gas welding the heat to melt the metal pieces and filler rod is provided by an oxyacetylene torch. The torch is so called because it burns acetylene gas with oxygen, at a temperature approaching 3,000°C. Arc welding, on the other hand, uses an electric arc – a kind of continuous spark – to produce a high temperature. The arc is struck by passing a heavy electric current between the metal to be joined and an electrode held by the welder.

In resistance welding two electrodes carrying heavy current pinch together two overlapping plates. The resistance to the passage of electricity between the two electrodes produces enough heat to fuse the metal in between. This creates a spot weld. When a circular electrode is used, a continuous seam weld is formed.

Brazing and soldering are alternative methods of joining metals. Brazing involves melting brass to form a joint; soldering does the same thing, only with melted solder.

▲ The former transatlantic liner *Queen Mary*, launched in 1934, is now a floating hotel and conference centre at Long Beach, Los Angeles, USA. Like most ships of its day, the 310.8-m long vessel is built of riveted steel plates.

▶ The huge Magnus oil-production rig just after construction. It was built by welding together sections of steel pipe, which measured 13 km long overall and weighed 14,000 tonnes. It is now sited in the Magnus oilfield off the Shetland Isles of Britain.

Machining

Most metal objects shaped by casting, forging or other methods need some kind of finishing treatment before they are ready for use. For example, they may need to have holes drilled or metal removed to bring them to the right size and shape. The machines that carry out such metal-finishing processes are known as machine tools. They play an important part in the modern assembly-line method of manufacturing because they can work to very accurate limits and produce near-identical parts.

Since machine tools are used to cut metal, they have powerful motors to drive the cutting tools. These tools are made from very hard tool steels, which retain their sharpness during machining. Special high-speed steels contain-

ing tungsten and chromium remain sharp even when they run red-hot. To help reduce temperatures during machining, the tool and workpiece are cooled by a light "cutting oil". This also helps lubricate the cutting operation.

The lathe

One of the most common machine tools in workshops is the lathe, on which a process called turning is carried out. On a lathe, a workpiece is rotated and various cutting tools are then moved in to cut it. The workpiece is rotated between a headstock at one end and a tailstock at the other. It is clamped in a chuck in the headstock, which also houses the motor that drives the chuck. A gearbox allows the

▲ Machinists examine a wing panel for a European Airbus, which is being cut to shape on a huge milling machine. Twin cutting heads are working on two panels. The wing panels on the Airbus are machined from solid metal. This method of construction is much stronger than conventional riveting.

▲ A lathe operator checks the diameter of a large turbine rotor with a gauge. The rotor was originally shaped on a hydraulic forging press. It is now being "turned" on a lathe, where metal will be removed until it is the right size. The chuck of the lathe is at the top; the tailstock is at the bottom.

workpiece to be driven at a number of speeds from, say, 20 to 2,000 revolutions per minute.

The cutting tools are mounted on a cross-slide, which in turn is mounted on a saddle. The saddle moves lengthwise along the lathe, while the cross-slide moves at right-angles to it, so as to carry the tools towards or away from the rotating workpiece. The cross-slide and the saddle both run on precision screw threads so that they can be positioned with great accuracy.

Drilling and milling

Another common machine tool is the drill press, which is used to drill holes. The workpiece is held stationary, while a rotating drill bit is lowered into it. The drill bit has cutting edges just at the tip and spiral grooves, or flutes, along the side. This allows the cut metal, known as swarf, to escape. Turret drills have a drill head that carries a number of drill bits of different sizes.

Milling is a machining operation carried out with a rotating toothed cutting wheel. Metal is removed as the workpiece moves past the wheel, which may rotate at speeds approaching 10,000 revolutions per minute.

Other machine tools carry out other metal-finishing operations. For example, a shaping machine uses a chisel-like tool to cut flat surfaces; a grinding machine uses a rotating abrasive wheel or a moving abrasive belt to remove metal.

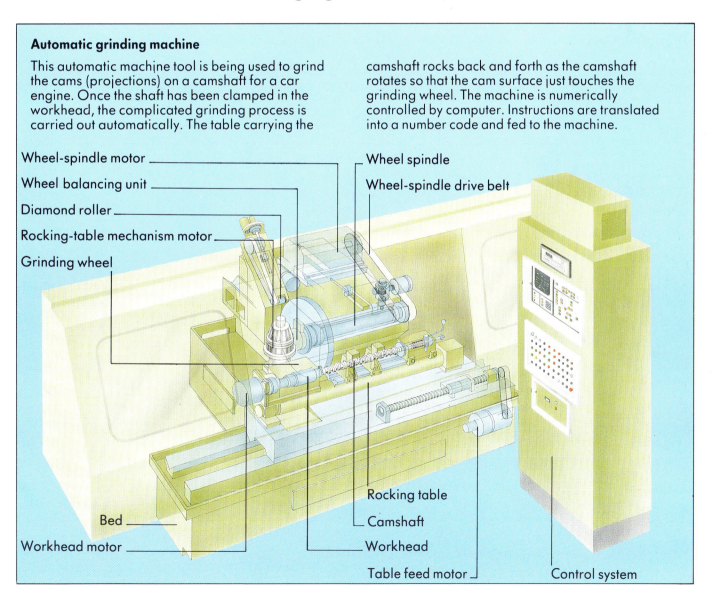

Automatic grinding machine

This automatic machine tool is being used to grind the cams (projections) on a camshaft for a car engine. Once the shaft has been clamped in the workhead, the complicated grinding process is carried out automatically. The table carrying the camshaft rocks back and forth as the camshaft rotates so that the cam surface just touches the grinding wheel. The machine is numerically controlled by computer. Instructions are translated into a number code and fed to the machine.

Wheel-spindle motor
Wheel balancing unit
Diamond roller
Rocking-table mechanism motor
Grinding wheel
Wheel spindle
Wheel-spindle drive belt
Bed
Workhead motor
Rocking table
Camshaft
Workhead
Table feed motor
Control system

The chemical industry

▶ A chemical engineer adjusts a valve regulating the flow of materials through a pilot plant. This is a small-scale chemical plant used for testing a new process. If it performs satisfactorily, d full-scale plant might be built.

From its beginnings in the 1700s, the chemical industry has grown into one of the largest industries there is. Its products, chemicals, are used in practically every other industry, from electronics to steelmaking. They are used in agriculture, for fertilizers and pesticides, and in the home, in paints, washing powders, hairsprays and medicines. And most of us use, wear, and even eat the products made from, or processed with, chemicals. These range from margarine and paper to drip-dry shirts and non-stick cookware.

The chemical industry uses processes devised in the chemistry laboratory. It transforms raw materials into finished chemical products, or else into intermediate chemicals that other manufacturers turn into products.

Chemical engineering

Chemical engineering is the branch of engineering which designs, builds and operates chemical plants, the factories in which chemicals are produced or processed.

Chemical engineers take a process from the chemistry laboratory and develop it on a large enough scale for industrial production. This is usually much more difficult than it sounds. For example, in the laboratory, heating a few millilitres of acid in a glass flask over a Bunsen burner presents few problems. But heating up thousands of litres of acid in an industrial plant is quite a different matter.

Each chemical manufacturing process uses raw materials and converts them into finished products. In this way, each process is different. However, every process involves a certain number of standard chemical and physical operations. Chemical engineers design suitable equipment to carry out these operations economically. Where possible, they use standard, rather than specially designed equipment, to keep down the cost.

Standard chemical operations are known as unit processes. They include oxidation, chlorination and hydrogenation, in which, respectively, oxygen, chlorine and hydrogen combine with other substances. Another important unit process is polymerization, in which small molecules are built up into larger ones.

Standard physical operations are known as unit operations. Common ones include mixing, filtering, distillation, evaporation and drying.

▶ A chemist works in a laboratory on a method of vacuum-processing materials. There is no guarantee that a large-scale plant would be able to repeat the process successfully or economically.

▼ The diagram shows a likely timescale for the nine main stages from the birth of an idea to the production of a saleable product. The whole process often takes more than five years from start to finish. It could take another five years for the plant to pay for itself.

| Project formulated | Process discovered | Process defined in laboratory | Small test plant built | Process defined in test plant | Sanction for full scale plant | Full scale plant designed and constructed | Plant commission and start-up | Plant on stream |

Time (months)

| 6 | 12 | 18 | 24 | 30 | 36 | 42 | 48 | 54 | 60 |

Heavy chemicals

The chemical industry produces vast tonnages of a wide range of chemicals. But a relatively small number of chemicals account for the bulk of production. These are generally called heavy chemicals, because they are produced in such large amounts. In contrast, some chemicals are produced only in small amounts. They are usually termed fine chemicals. They are also often the product of more complex chemical processing. Dyes and pharmaceuticals, or drugs, are examples of fine chemicals.

Most of the leading heavy chemicals are inorganic. They are made from salts, minerals or gases in the air. Among the most important are sulphuric acid, ammonia, sodium hydroxide and sodium carbonate. Sulphuric acid is vital to so many modern manufacturing processes that it is often called the "lifeblood of industry". But the other three chemicals mentioned are also vital to modern industry.

Early chemical industry

The modern chemical industry began in the 1790s. That is when Nicolas Leblanc, a French surgeon turned chemist, found a way of making sodium carbonate on an industrial scale. The chemical was much in demand for making soap and glass. The first stage of the Leblanc process was to treat sodium chloride (common salt) with sulphuric acid. The demand for sulphuric acid for the Leblanc process led in turn to an improved process for making the acid, called the lead-chamber process. This was later superseded by the present method, which is called the contact process.

Salt water is the starting point for the modern method of making sodium carbonate. This is called the ammonia-soda process because it involves a series of reactions with ammonia. Salt water is also the raw material for making caustic soda, or sodium hydroxide. But this time no lengthy series of chemical reactions is involved. Caustic soda is produced simply by passing an electric current through the salt water. This method, electrolysis, is a useful way of producing many metals and chemicals.

▶ This plant makes ammonia by combining nitrogen and hydrogen in the presence of an iron-oxide catalyst. The process, called the Haber synthesis, takes place at about 400°C and at a pressure of up to 1,000 atmospheres.

Making sulphuric acid

Sulphur is the usual starting point in the manufacture of sulphuric acid. It is heated with air in a furnace and oxidized to sulphur dioxide gas. After being cooled in a heat exchanger, the gas is fed to a converter. There, with the help of a catalyst, it is further oxidized to sulphur trioxide gas. This gas is absorbed by a spray of dilute sulphuric acid. Concentrated acid results.

Heat exchange
Furnace
Sulphur
Steam
Water
SO_2
Waste gas
Sulphuric acid
Vent to atmosphere
Dry air
SO_2
Converter
Absorber
SO_3
Concentrated Sulphuric acid

► The main uses of four of the world's leading industrial chemicals. A major use of sulphuric acid and ammonia is to make fertilizers. The acid is used to make superphosphate; ammonia is used to make ammonium nitrate and urea. Caustic soda, or sodium hydroxide, is used for making soap, paper and artificial silks. One of sodium carbonate's most useful applications is in the manufacture of glass.

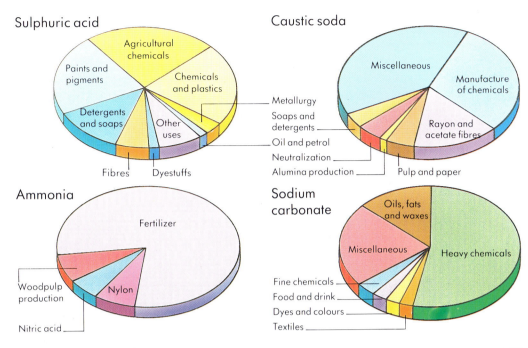

Sulphuric acid

Agricultural chemicals
Paints and pigments
Chemicals and plastics
Detergents and soaps
Other uses
Metallurgy
Soaps and detergents
Oil and petrol
Fibres
Dyestuffs

Caustic soda

Miscellaneous
Manufacture of chemicals
Rayon and acetate fibres
Neutralization
Alumina production
Pulp and paper

Ammonia

Fertilizer
Woodpulp production
Nylon
Nitric acid

Sodium carbonate

Oils, fats and waxes
Miscellaneous
Heavy chemicals
Fine chemicals
Food and drink
Dyes and colours
Textiles

Plastics

Plastics are now close to metals in being the most important industrial products of our age. We can define a plastic as a substance which has a long-chain molecule, and which can be moulded into shape when heated.

It is the long-chain molecules of plastics that make them so special. Most ordinary substances have short molecules, with just a few atoms linked together. Plastics, however, have long molecules containing thousands of atoms, almost always with a "backbone" of linked carbon atoms. Carbon is the only element that can link together in this way.

The raw materials for most plastics are hydrocarbons obtained from oil refining. The most useful of these is the gas ethylene (ethene). This has a short molecule with a backbone of just two carbon atoms. However, at high temperature and pressure, thousands of the short ethylene molecules will link together to form a long-chain molecule. We call ethylene a monomer ("one part"); the long-chain molecule, a polymer ("many parts"); and the process, polymerization. We know this particular polymer as polyethylene, or the material polythene.

Thousands of plastics can be produced by the polymerization of suitable hydrocarbons or their derivatives. Among other well-known plastics are PVC (polyvinyl chloride), nylon, polypropylene and polystyrene. All these plastics will soften when reheated. They are known as thermosoftening plastics, or thermoplastics. The other main group of plastics set rigid when they are heat-moulded into shape and will not soften when reheated. They are called thermosetting plastics, or thermosets. They include the original synthetic plastic, bakelite (phenol-formaldehyde), and its relatives urea- and melamine-formaldehyde.

▲ Like other modern cars, this MGB Roadster uses many different kinds of plastics. The tyres are made from synthetic rubber, as are the shock-absorbing bumpers. The paint was made using plastic resins, while the upholstery and carpets are woven from synthetic fibres. The hood is made from PVC, textured to imitate leather.

► A reservoir on Tenerife, in the Canary Islands, which has been lined with PVC.

Synthetic rubber

Many products used today are made from synthetic rubbers. They are a kind of "elastic plastic", a material called an elastomer. The search for a substitute for rubber led German chemists to produce the first successful synthetic rubber in 1927. Called buna rubber, it was made from butadiene, a chemical closely related to isoprene, the monomer in the sap of the rubber tree.

The most common synthetic rubber today is a copolymer (mixed polymer) of butadiene and styrene. Neoprene is a synthetic rubber made from acetylene (ethyne). It was one of the first to be discovered, by Wallace H. Carothers in 1928, and is still widely used because of its excellent resistance to high temperatures, oils and chemicals.

Shaping plastics

By far the commonest methods of shaping plastics involve moulding. Thermoplastics such as polyethylene and PVC are easy to mould into shape, and various methods are possible. Bowls, for example, are made by injection moulding. This involves heating the plastic until it is molten and then injecting it into a shaped, water-cooled mould.

Bottles and hollow toys can be made by blow moulding. A blob of molten plastic is delivered into a hollow mould, and then air is blown into it through a pipe. The plastic is forced against the mould and takes its shape.

Thermosetting plastics, such as bakelite, have to be shaped by a different technique, called compression moulding. They cannot be shaped like thermoplastics because they melt and set more or less at the same time. During their manufacture, the polymerization process is halted before the molecules begin to crosslink and set hard. This produces a so-called moulding resin. Objects such as cups are shaped when this resin is simultaneously heated and compressed in a mould.

Plastics can also be shaped by extrusion and laminating. Pipes, for example, are made by extrusion. A screw-like device forces molten plastic through the hole in a die. Plastic sheet is made by extruding molten plastic through a ring-shaped slit. Heatproof surfaces are made by laminating: sandwiching together layers of material soaked in thermosetting plastic resin.

Vacuum forming

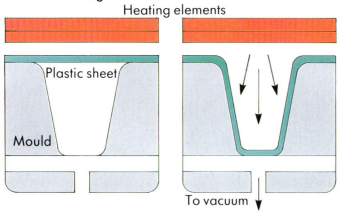

A sheet of plastic is placed on top of the mould and heated until it is soft. The mould is then connected to a vacuum line, and the air is sucked out of it. Outside air pressure forces the plastic into the mould.

Blow moulding

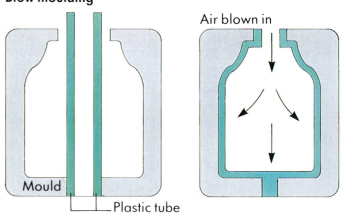

A length of hot plastic tubing is placed in the open mould. This then closes and seals the bottom. Air is blown into the tube from above, forcing the plastic against the walls of the mould.

Injection moulding

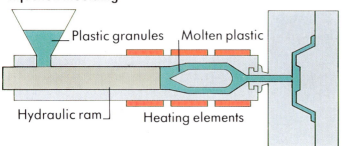

Plastic granules are fed into the injection-moulding machine and heated until they melt. A hydraulic ram then forces the molten plastic into the water-cooled mould, where it cools and sets.

Extrusion

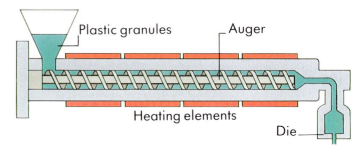

In the extrusion machine, plastic granules are heated until they melt. A screw-like device called an auger rotates and forces the molten plastic through a shaped hole called a die.

Man-made fibres

Silk, the finest natural fibre, is produced, or "spun", by the silkworm. In 1884 a French chemist, Hilaire Chardonnet, succeeded in imitating the silkworm and produced long fibres of what he called artificial silk. The material he used was cellulose nitrate. To make the fibres, he dissolved it in a solvent. He then forced the solution through the fine holes of a device similar to the spinning gland of the silkworm. Fibres formed when the solvent evaporated from the fine streams of solution.

In 1892 a better method of making artificial silk was developed, called the viscose process. It produced fibres of pure cellulose. This process is still very important today, producing fibres called viscose, or viscose rayon. The method involves treating the cellulose first with caustic soda and then with carbon disulphide. Fibres form when cellulose solution is pumped through a spinneret into an acid bath. In the bath the cellulose is regenerated. Acetate and triacetate are similar fibres made from cellulose acetates.

Many fibres used today, however, are wholly synthetic. They are kinds of plastics that can be drawn out into continuous threads, or filaments. Synthetic fibres are very strong, do not rot or absorb water, and are not attacked by insects. Among the best-known are nylon, polyester and acrylic fibres. Nylon and polyester fibres are produced by melt spinning: forcing molten plastic through a spinneret. The acrylics are produced from a solution of the plastic.

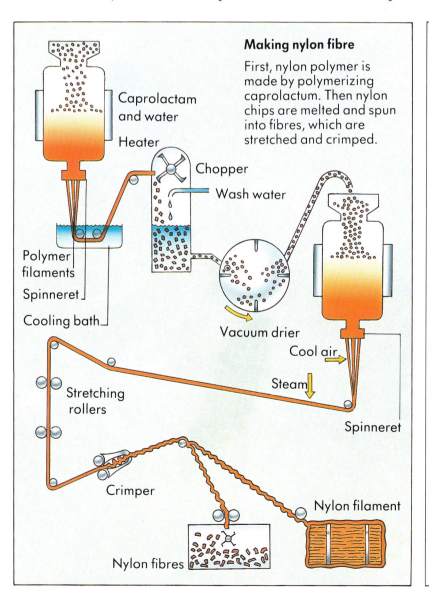

Making nylon fibre

First, nylon polymer is made by polymerizing caprolactum. Then nylon chips are melted and spun into fibres, which are stretched and crimped.

Caprolactam and water
Heater
Chopper
Wash water
Polymer filaments
Spinneret
Cooling bath
Vacuum drier
Cool air
Steam
Stretching rollers
Spinneret
Crimper
Nylon filament
Nylon fibres

The nylon man

In the early 1930s an American chemist, Wallace H. Carothers, headed a research team trying to find a substitute for silk. Carothers eventually found two coal-tar chemicals, adipic acid and hexamethylene-diamine, that would copolymerize to form molecules like those of silk. He produced the first practical fibre from the polymer in 1935. It was the first synthetic fibre, which was fine and lustrous, elastic and strong. It came to be called nylon.

Food and drugs

Chemical processing plays a major part in the daily lives of most people in developed countries. Farmers apply chemical fertilizers to the soil to make their crops grow better and produce greater yields. They spray the crops with chemicals to kill insects and protect them from disease. Our food is often treated with chemicals so that it looks and tastes more appetizing, and can be kept for longer periods without deteriorating. Methods of food preservation enable us to enjoy a wider range of foods. Without the benefit of man-made drugs, we would succumb to all manner of diseases.

► A doctor injects a drug into a patient with a hypodermic syringe. The body of the syringe carries a graduated scale, allowing an accurate dose of the drug to be administered. A subcutaneous injection goes under the skin. An intravenous injection, such as this, goes into a vein.

Agricultural chemicals

When crops grow, they extract nutrients from the soil. To ensure that the soil remains fertile, these nutrients must be replaced. This is done by applying fertilizers. In the early days of farming, animal manure was enough. Nowadays chemical fertilizers, such as superphosphate and ammonium compounds, are used.

Growing crops can be attacked by many insect pests and also many fungal diseases. Again, the chemist comes to the aid of the farmer by creating powerful insecticides and fungicides. Competition with weeds is also eliminated by means of herbicides (weed-killers). Many of the most potent pesticides are chlorinated hydrocarbons, such as dieldrin and DDT. These chemicals are deadly to animal life, and once in the food chain, their effects accumulate. Other effective pesticides, including organic phosphorus compounds, are less toxic to animal life and are not so persistent.

◄ Chemical herbicide has been sprayed around this young oil palm to kill weed growth. This allows the palm room to establish itself.

▼ An Asian farmer sprays insecticide on a cereal crop to prevent insect pests breeding and multiplying.

Food technology

Most of the foods we eat have been processed in some way. Even fresh foods such as fruits may have been treated with chemicals to assist ripening. Food processing began thousands of years ago, when early peoples began to make bread from the grain crops they gathered. Bread is still one of the basic foodstuffs of the world, and has been called the "staff of life".

The principles of making bread have hardly changed over the years, although it is now often mass-produced in factories. Bread is made by baking a prepared dough in a hot oven. The dough is a mixture of flour, salt and water, to which yeast has been added to make it ferment. The fermenting yeast produces carbon dioxide gas, which makes the dough rise. This gives

bread its typical light texture when it is baked.

From early times also fermentation has been used for another purpose, making beer. Beer is produced by fermenting watery mixtures of grains. The yeast turns sugar extracted from the grain into alcohol, while carbon dioxide is given off as a waste product. This reaction was probably the first chemical process utilized by man.

Like bread, milk has been part of our staple diet since the beginning of civilization. And it has also been processed into other foodstuffs for nearly as long. One is butter. This is made by churning the cream that settles on top of the milk. Churning – rotating the cream in a drum – causes the little fat globules in the cream to join together into a solid mass, butter. Cheese is another food derived from milk. It is made by adding rennet to milk, which makes it set into a solid curd. This then matures into cheese.

▼ Fermentation tanks at a distillery. In these tanks sugars extracted from grain are fermented with yeast. The yeast changes the sugars into alcohol, with carbon dioxide bubbling off as a waste product.

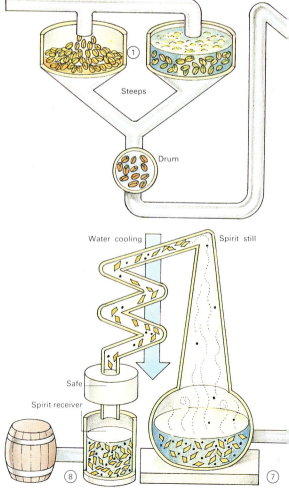

We can think of cheesemaking as a way of preserving milk, which otherwise "goes off", or turns sour, in a day or so. It would go off even sooner were it not for a treatment it receives in the dairy before bottling or packaging. This treatment is pasteurization, which involves the milk being heated briefly, then quickly cooled.

Several other methods are used to preserve food. They all aim to halt or slow down the processes that cause food to spoil. Spoilage may be brought about by microorganisms, such as bacteria, or by chemical changes. Traditional methods of preservation include smoking, pickling and drying. The commonest methods of preservation are canning and freezing.

▶ Filling cans with fish in a canning factory. The cans will next be sealed, and then sterilized by heating in batches.

Making malt whisky

The making of malt Scotch whisky is a lengthy process. The first step is malting, which involves soaking barley until it germinates, or starts to shoot (1). The malted barley is then dried in a kiln (2). After being weighed, the dried barley is ground up (3) and mixed with hot water to form mash (4). The sugar (maltose) in the grain passes into solution to form a liquid called wort. After filtering and cooling, the wort is fermented with yeast (5) for about two days. The liquid is then distilled (6), producing a weak alcohol and water solution. This solution is distilled again (7), producing a "spirit" with a high alcoholic content (8).

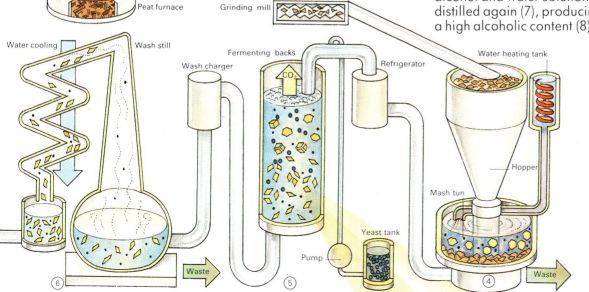

Malt kiln
Malt bins
Water
Smoke
Dressing machine
Waste
Weighing machine
Peat furnace
Grinding mill

Water cooling
Wash still
Fermenting backs
Wash charger
CO_2
Refrigerator
Water heating tank
Hopper
Mash tun
Yeast tank
Pump
Waste
Waste
Waste

Barley
Germinated barley
Malted barley
Peat smoke
Malt grist
Sugar (Maltose)
Yeast
Alcohol (ethanol)

Synthetic foods

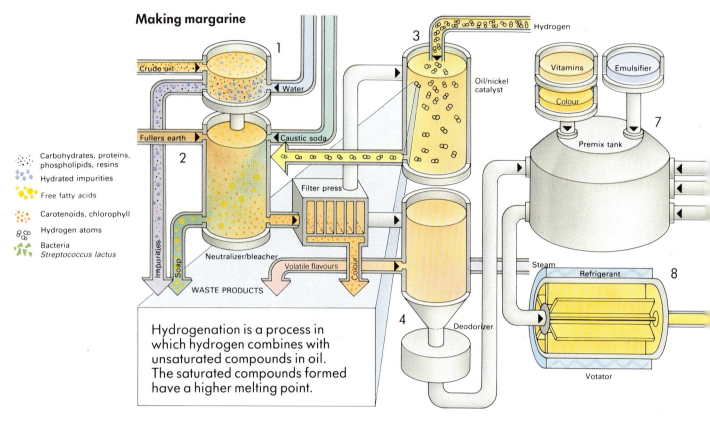

Making margarine

1

Crude oil
Water

Fullers earth

2

Caustic soda

3

Hydrogen

Oil/nickel catalyst

Vitamins
Emulsifier
Colour

Premix tank

7

Filter press

Neutralizer/bleacher

Impurities
Soap

WASTE PRODUCTS

Volatile flavours
Colour

4

Deodorizer

Steam
Refrigerant

8

Votator

- ∷ Carbohydrates, proteins, phospholipids, resins
- Hydrated impurities
- Free fatty acids
- Carotenoids, chlorophyll
- Hydrogen atoms
- Bacteria *Streptococcus lactus*

Hydrogenation is a process in which hydrogen combines with unsaturated compounds in oil. The saturated compounds formed have a higher melting point.

In 1869 a French chemist named Hippolyte Mège-Mouriès patented one of the first synthetic foods. He called it margarine, a name loosely based on his surname. It won him a contest launched by Emperor Napoleon III to find a palatable substitute for butter. Mège-Mouriès made his margarine using fats from beef suet, pig's stomach and cow's udder. He mixed with them skimmed milk, or whey.

Animal fats are still used to make some margarines. But most are made using vegetable oils, including safflower, sunflower, coconut and palm oils. These oils are converted during manufacture into solid fats by treatment with hydrogen. Margarines based on vegetable oils now sell very well because it is believed that they are healthier to eat than butter and other animal fat products.

Margarine contains various additives which give it the right consistency, improve its nutritional value, help preserve it and enhance its appearance. They include emulsifiers, which prevent the fats and water in the margarine separating out. An important emulsifier is lecithin, found in egg yolks. Vitamins A and D may be added to increase the food value.

The colour in margarines comes from a dye called beta-carotene, which occurs naturally in carrots. But most of this colouring is now made synthetically from coal tar. Potassium sorbate is a common preservative found in margarines.

Emulsifiers, vitamins, colouring and preservatives are common additives found in most processed foods today. Other additives include thickeners, such as gelatine and alginates (extracted from seaweed), and anti-oxidants. These are mainly synthetic compounds that stop fats going rancid and other foods developing unpleasant flavours. Monosodium glutamate is a common additive that brings out the flavour of food. Sweetness is provided by the addition of glucose or other sugars, or by synthetic sweeteners such as aspartame and saccharin.

Synthetic proteins include meat substitutes, properly called texturized vegetable protein (TVP). The vegetable involved is the soya bean. Protein is extracted from the beans and then dissolved in alkali. The solution is then extruded through a spinneret into an acid bath. The protein comes out of solution as fibres, which are gathered into a rope and then chopped.

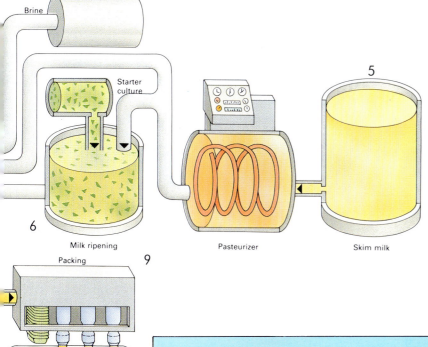

Brine

Starter culture

6
Milk ripening

Pasteurizer

5
Skim milk

Packing
9

◀ Margarine is now made mainly from vegetable oil. The impure, or crude oil is washed with water (1) and then treated with caustic soda and Fuller's earth (2). The alkali combines with unwanted substances to form a soap. The Fuller's earth removes colour. Some oils require treatment with hydrogen to make them solid (3). Steam is then bubbled through the purified oil in a deodorizer (4) to remove any remaining odour. Meanwhile, skimmed milk is being prepared in another part of the plant (5). After being pasteurized, it is "ripened" by treatment with bacteria (6). It then passes with the oil and brine into the premix tank (7). Other ingredients are also added at this stage. These may include colourings, to give a "buttery" colour; vitamins, to improve its food value; and an emulsifier. The margarine mixture solidifies in a refrigerated rotating device called a votator (8) and passes to the packing machine (9).

Menthol

Solvent

Methyl acetate

Menthone

Iso menthone
Menthofuran

Octan-3-ol

The food chemist

Chemists help food manufacturers ensure that their products look good, taste good, have a long shelf-life and, above all, are safe. Food chemists (inset) study, for example, how the body recognizes flavours and the mechanisms of food decay. They develop additives to improve flavour, arrest decay, and so on.

They also analyse natural flavourings and try to imitate them or improve upon them by chemical synthesis. In their analysis they often use a technique called chromatography to separate out the chemicals in a substance. An analysis of natural peppermint oil (left) shows that menthol, menthone and methyl acetate are the main ingredients. A mixture of these chemicals would produce an artificial peppermint flavour that is very similar to that of the natural product.

In many countries all additives in food products must be listed on the label. In Europe they are usually identified by an E number, which indicates that they have been approved for use in EEC (European Economic Community) countries.

Making drugs

Penicillin

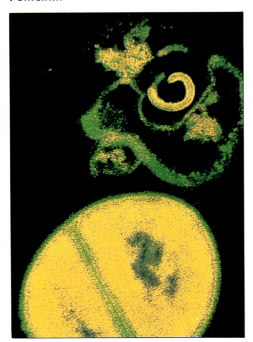

The original antibiotic, penicillin, is produced by the *Penicillium* mould. It is still widely used to combat diseases caused by such bacteria as staphylococcus, which causes boils and abcesses. The picture shows at bottom a normal staphylococcus bacterium, and at top a bacterium that has been destroyed by penicillin. Penicillin works by breaking up the bacterium's outer membrane.

◄ Traditionally, drugs were prepared using minerals and plant extracts. Some such as tincture of iodine and digitalis (from foxgloves), are still used. But most medicines are now manufactured.

▲ Opium poppies growing in Thailand. It is harvested by cutting the pods and collecting the liquid that oozes out (inset). The pain-killing properties of opium have been known for over 2,000 years.

► A technician tends a fermentation vessel in a biotechnology plant, which produces disease-fighting antibodies from cultured cells. These antibodies are used to help diagnose diseases.

Today doctors have at their disposal a vast array of medicines, or drugs, with which they can successfully treat most of the diseases that affect us. Drugs are also known as pharmaceuticals. They may be derived from plants, animals and minerals, or made from chemicals.

Opium, obtained from poppy seeds, is probably the oldest known effective drug. Opium and drugs made from it – codeine, morphine and heroin – are powerful analgesics, or pain-relievers. But they are highly addictive. This means that people who take them regularly develop a craving for them, and find it very hard to stop taking them.

Quinine is a well-known plant drug, used to treat malaria. It was obtained originally from the bark of the cinchona tree of South America. But most is now manufactured synthetically.

The manufacture of synthetic drugs dates from the late 1890s, when the Bayer chemical company in Germany began manufacturing aspirin on a large scale from coal-tar chemicals. Among other powerful synthetic drugs, the sulphonamides, or sulpha drugs, are outstanding. They fight many bacterial infections.

Among drugs obtained from animals, the hormone insulin is best known. It is extracted from the pancreas of cattle and pigs, and is used to treat diabetes.

Antibiotics are perhaps the most powerful weapons against disease. Alexander Fleming discovered the original antibiotic, penicillin, in 1928. It went into widespread production in the early 1940s. The antibiotics can now treat diseases such as pneumonia and typhoid, which in the past were generally fatal.

Everyday industries

The invention of paper in China in about AD 105 can be considered a key invention in the development of civilization. It provided, in the course of time, our first means of mass communication and mass education through books, newspapers and magazines.

Spinning and weaving are two of the most ancient crafts, dating back at least 10,000 years. Until about 200 years ago, they were practised at home on simple machines, such as the spinning wheel and hand loom. In many countries, they still are. Then in the 1700s more productive spinning and weaving machines were invented. These took textile-making out of the home, and it became the first factory industry.

▶ Machines in a modern factory work automatically under the control of a computer, or "electronic brain". Individual machines may even have their own "brains", in the guise of a silicon chip.

Pulp and paper

Until about 150 years ago, most paper was made from linen and rags, materials that are still used to make the best-quality writing paper. But increasing demand for paper, for books and newspapers, led to wood in the form of woodpulp becoming the main raw material.

Woodpulp is made mainly from softwoods such as pine and spruces. It can be made in two ways. Mechanical pulp is made by shredding logs in a huge grinding machine. This results in a coarse pulp suitable only for making newsprint, the paper on which newspapers are printed. Chemical pulp is used to produce better quality paper. It is made by "digesting" wood chips in a solution of chemicals, usually sodium sulphate. The chemical treatment frees the wood fibres from their binder (lignin).

Woodpulp is usually transported to the paper-mill as dry bales. And so the first stage in papermaking is to mix the pulp with water to convert it back into a liquid state. The liquid pulp then feeds into a machine in which sets of revolving knives beat and fray the wood fibres. This enables them to bind together better later.

Next, the beaten pulp goes into a mixer tank, where it is blended with materials that will determine the quality and appearance of the finished paper. They include a filler, such as china clay, to give the paper "body" and make it smoother; size or resin glue to make the paper easier to write and print on; and maybe dyes or pigments to add colour.

The prepared watery pulp then passes to the papermaking machine, the Fourdrinier machine. It flows on to a wire-mesh belt, where the water drains or is sucked away. The damp web that forms is then squeezed by heavy rollers before being fed round steam-heated cylinders to dry. After a final rolling by heavy calendar rolls, the paper is wound on to reels.

Papermaking

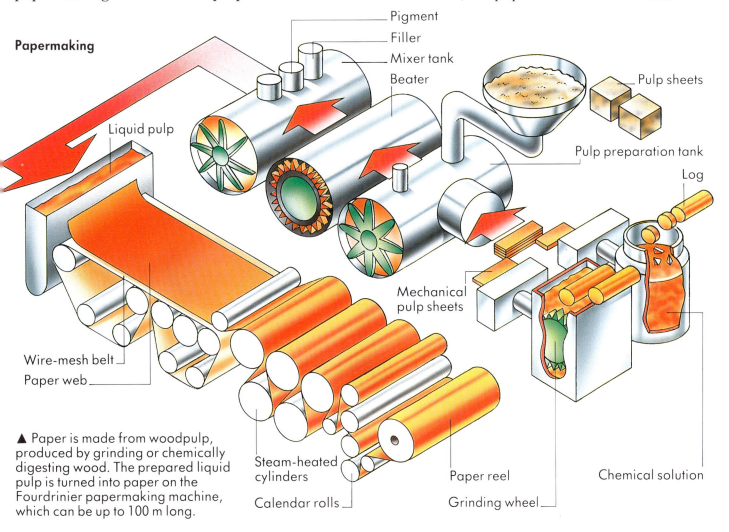

Pigment
Filler
Mixer tank
Beater
Pulp sheets
Liquid pulp
Pulp preparation tank
Log
Mechanical pulp sheets
Wire-mesh belt
Paper web
Steam-heated cylinders
Calendar rolls
Paper reel
Grinding wheel
Chemical solution

▲ Paper is made from woodpulp, produced by grinding or chemically digesting wood. The prepared liquid pulp is turned into paper on the Fourdrinier papermaking machine, which can be up to 100 m long.

Textiles

Textiles are any materials made from fibres. The most common material is cloth, made by weaving long threads, called yarns. Yarn is made by drawing out and twisting "ropes" of fibres, a process called spinning.

The traditional fibres for making cloth come from animals and plants. More and more these days, however, synthetic fibres are used instead. They are made by processing natural materials, such as cellulose, or are manufactured wholly from chemicals.

The original fibre used was wool, which comes from the fleece of sheep. It is a kind of hair that is naturally curly. The Merino breed produces the finest wool and the heaviest fleece. The fleeces of some goats, such as the Angora and Cashmere breeds, also yield excellent fibres.

Another prized animal fibre, silk, has quite a different origin. It is produced by the silkworm, the larva stage of a moth. Unlike other natural fibres, which are short, silk is produced as a continuous thread, or filament.

Cotton is by far the most important plant fibre, obtained from the boll, or fluffy seed-head of the cotton plant. Flax is a grass-like plant that has fibres in its stem. They are made into the fabric we call linen. Other natural fibres include jute and asbestos.

Spinning

With the exception of silk, the fibres from plants and animals are relatively short, usually just a few centimetres long. To make them suitable for making textiles, they must be spun into continuous yarn. Before the actual spinning process can begin, the fibres must be carefully prepared.

In the case of cotton, the bales are first opened out and the fluffy bolls are broken down into a loose fibre blanket called lap. This is then fed into a carding engine, which removes the very short fibres and also straightens out the long ones. For the best-quality yarn the fibres are straightened further by combing. They emerge from the combing machine as a web, which is then gathered into a loose rope, called sliver. Several slivers are combined and drawn out through rotating rollers to form roving. The roving goes to the spinning frames, where they are drawn out and given a twist for strength.

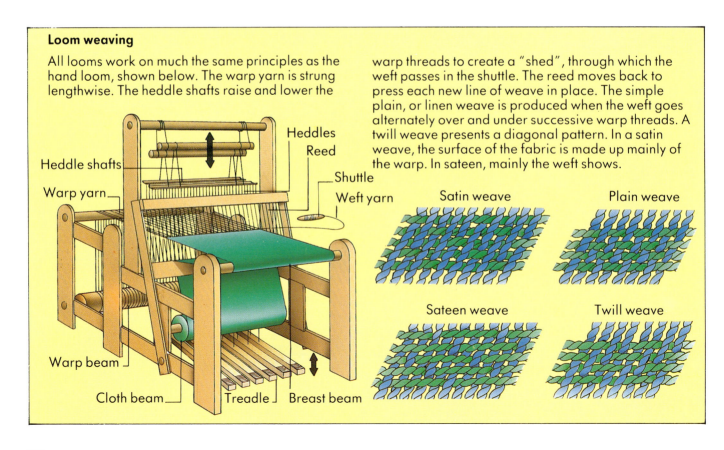

Loom weaving

All looms work on much the same principles as the hand loom, shown below. The warp yarn is strung lengthwise. The heddle shafts raise and lower the warp threads to create a "shed", through which the weft passes in the shuttle. The reed moves back to press each new line of weave in place. The simple plain, or linen weave is produced when the weft goes alternately over and under successive warp threads. A twill weave presents a diagonal pattern. In a satin weave, the surface of the fabric is made up mainly of the warp. In sateen, mainly the weft shows.

Heddles
Reed
Heddle shafts
Warp yarn
Shuttle
Weft yarn
Warp beam
Cloth beam
Treadle
Breast beam

Satin weave
Plain weave
Sateen weave
Twill weave

Weaving

Weaving takes place on a loom, on which one set of threads (the warp) is stretched lengthwise on a frame. The weaving process consists of passing thread (the weft) crosswise through a gap (the shed), created by raising and lowering sets of warp threads. Different patterns of weave are produced according to how the warp threads are separated. On traditional looms the weft is carried through the warp in a shuttle. But in the latest looms, rapier-like rods and even jets of air or water are used to carry the weft. On some of these looms, over 400 m of weft can be put down each minute.

Dazzling dyes

Textiles have been made more attractive by dyeing for at least 5,000 years. Until the mid-1800s textile manufacturers had to rely on natural dyes, extracted mainly from plants.

In 1856, however, the English chemist William H. Perkin accidentally produced a new dye while experimenting with aniline, a liquid extracted then from coal tar. He called the new dye mauveine, which had the colour we now call mauve (see picture). It was the first synthetic dye.

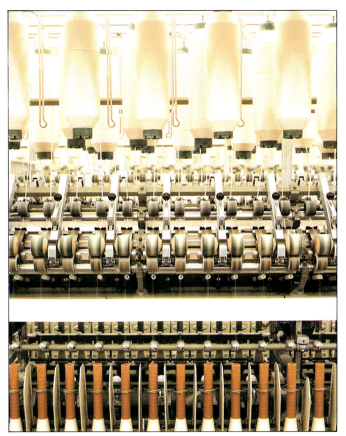

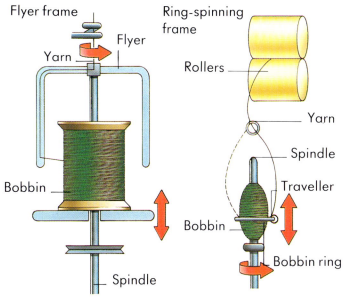

Flyer frame
Flyer
Yarn
Bobbin
Spindle

Ring-spinning frame
Rollers
Yarn
Spindle
Traveller
Bobbin
Bobbin ring

▲ (top) The final stage of spinning worsted yarn. Worsted is produced using only long wool fibres. Two common spinning machines are the flyer and ring-spinning frames (bottom). On the flyer frame, the yarn is twisted as the flyer spins round at high speed, dragging the bobbin with it. On the ring-spinning frame drawn-out yarn is wound on to the bobbin and given a twist as the traveller moves round the ring.

Transport

The revolution in industry began in textile manufacturing, and gathered pace at the end of the 1700s. Throughout the 1800s, transport also underwent a revolution. First came the railways, on which new locomotives could haul enormous loads. These locomotives had engines powered by steam. Steam engines also took to the water, making shipping faster and more reliable.

By the end of the 1800s, road transport began to improve, with the development of the motor car. Air transport, in the form of balloons and airships, had also begun. But the real breakthrough in air transport came when the Wright brothers in the United States built the first power-driven aeroplane in 1903.

Transport by water tends to be very slow, because of friction with the water. In general, ships today are not much faster than they were a century ago. Hovercraft and hydrofoils are new kinds of vessels which have been successful in increasing the speed of transport over water. They are only used on short trips, however.

In traditional shipbuilding, hulls are usually constructed from steel plates welded together. The hull is not built up plate by plate. Large sections are built first and then put together afterwards. Glass-reinforced plastic and even concrete hulls are also made.

Railway construction has not changed much since the pioneering days of the last century. The idea of running a steel-wheeled vehicle on a steel track is a good one because of the low friction between them. Modern rails are made by rolling steel slabs with grooved rollers. The biggest change in railway practice since the last century is in the power source for the locomotives. Most are now powered by diesel engines or electricity.

The motor car, however, has changed almost

The international Airbus

The succesful European Airbus is manufactured piecemeal in plants spread throughout Europe. In Britain, British Aerospace makes the wings (left); in France, SNECMA assembles American-designed engines and Aérospatiale makes the nose and cockpit; in Germany MBB makes the fuselage and tail fin; in the Netherlands, Fokker makes the movable surfaces on the wings (flaps, airbrakes and so on); and in Spain, CASA makes the tailplane.

All the prefabricated units are transported to Aérospatiale's plant at Toulouse in south-west France, where they are assembled on a production line (right). The larger parts are delivered by the bulbous Super Guppy.

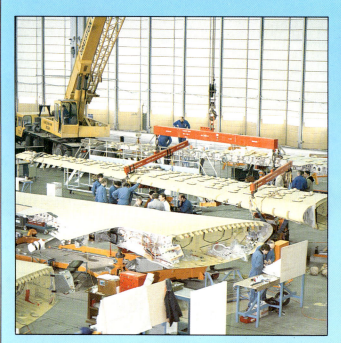

beyond recognition. Its success of the car has been a triumph for manufacturing industry. The early cars were built by hand in small numbers. Today's cars are produced in their millions. Mass-production was pioneered by car-makers. They were the first to introduce assembly lines, automation and robots.

Whereas most ships, locomotives and cars are constructed mainly in steel, most aircraft are built of aluminium alloys. These alloys are as strong as steel, but very much lighter. The aluminium sheets and other structures in the airframe, or aircraft body, are put together mainly by riveting. The method of construction, termed "fail-safe", uses staggered joints and other devices to prevent dangerous cracks running through the structure. Synthetic adhesives are also being used in airframe construction. Even the fuselage of some aircraft is now made of synthetic composites.

▶ Robot machines weld together steel sections to form the body shells on a car production line. Robot welders work with greater precision than humans, and are not affected by the heat and glare.

▼ The main hull and deck structure of a ship nearing completion at Ancona in Italy. Like all big ships, it is constructed of welded steel plates. When the hull is finished and painted, the ship will be ready to launch.

Electronics

Electronics is concerned with devices that control the flow of electrons in substances. It puts electrons to work in various ways. For example, it makes them create pictures on a TV screen, carry out sums in a calculator, work a computer, guide a robot and play a compact disc.

Electronics deals with the flow of electricity not so much through wires, but through substances that hardly conduct electricity at all. We call them semiconductors. The most important semiconductor by far is silicon. This element does not conduct electricity at all when it is pure, but it does – a little – when tiny amounts of impurities are added to it.

By adding different impurities to it, silicon can be given two electrical states, called n-type and p-type. By linking bits of the two types together, electronic devices like transistors, capacitors and resistors can be made. And they can be linked, or integrated, into circuits that can work TVs, calculators or computers.

There has been a revolution in electronics during the last few decades because these integrated circuits can now be made microscopically small. A tiny wafer of silicon the size of a shirt-button can carry hundreds of thousands of components and by itself run computers and other electronic equipment. We call these wafers silicon chips or microchips. A typical chip is only about 6 mm square and about one-tenth of a millimetre thick, and it weighs less than one-hundredth of a gram.

Making chips

A chip is designed so that its components and circuits can be built up in layers. There are layers of n-type and p-type silicon; a number of

▲ A Tiger beetle holds a microchip in its jaws. Beetle-sized chips like this are the "brains" behind today's home computers.

▶ Designers working on oversize layouts of the circuits for a silicon chip. A separate layout is needed for each layer of the chip. Designers use computers to design the layouts, and make changes to them by means of light-pens when the circuits are displayed on a video display unit.

conducting and insulating layers; and a final metallic layer (usually aluminium) to provide connections. The components and pathways between them are required only in certain parts of each layer. So the other areas have to be masked off. Masks are made for each layer by photographically reducing a circuit layout 250 times its real size.

The starting point for making chips is a slice of ultrapure silicon crystal about 15 cm across. This has space for several hundred chips. The first stage of processing is to treat, or "dope", the slice with chemical vapour (often boron) to create p-type silicon. The slice is then heated in a steam oven to give it an insulating layer of silicon dioxide.

A series of photographic masking and etching processes then follow, one for each layer. They create "windows" through which the silicon can

be treated. In the first masking stage, for example, areas of silicon dioxide are stripped away to allow doping of the silicon by phosphorus vapour, which creates n-type regions.

In all, more than two dozen stages of masking, doping, etching and so on, are required in making chips. Afterwards, each chip on the slice is carefully tested and inspected. As many as one in four may be rejected as a result.

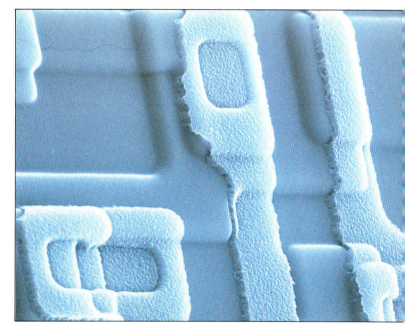

▶ A small section of the circuitry on a silicon chip, magnified about 4,000 times.

▼ Slices of silicon containing finished chips being inspected under the microscope. Next, they will be cut up, and the good chips will go for mounting. Many will be rejected.

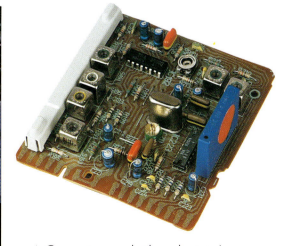

▲ Computers and other electronic equipment are assembled from circuit boards like this. The various electronic components are mounted on an insulated board and connected by printed circuits, made up of films of copper. This method of assembly simplifies fault-finding.

Glossary

acetate A form of rayon in which the fibres are of cellulose acetate or triacetate.

antibiotic A compound produced by a microorganism, such as a mould, which can kill bacteria that cause disease.

assembly line A method of production in which workers add parts to a product as it moves past them on a conveyor.

automation The widespread introduction of automatic machines to industry.

bakelite The first synthetic plastic, named after its inventor, Leo H. Baekeland.

biotechnology Methods of producing biological materials such as antibiotics on an industrial scale.

blow moulding A method of shaping hollow plastic objects by blowing air into the middle of molten plastic within a mould.

brazing A method of joining metal parts by melting brass in between them.

casting A method of shaping metal by pouring it as a red-hot liquid into a mould and allowing it to cool.

catalyst A substance that increases (or decreases) the rate of a chemical reaction without changing chemically itself.

compression moulding A method of shaping thermosetting plastics by the simultaneous application of heat and pressure.

copolymer A polymer made from different monomers. The commonest synthetic rubber is made of a copolymer of butadiene and styrene.

cracking An oil-refinery process in which heavy oil fractions are broken down into lighter, more useful ones. It may be brought about with the help of a catalyst or steam. Steam cracking produces a wide variety of chemical raw materials.

DDT The compound dichloro-diphenyl-trichloroethane, a powerful insecticide. Its use is now restricted because it is toxic to higher forms of life and is very persistent – it remains in the environment for a long time.

die A metal mould.

diecasting Casting molten metal into shape in a metal mould, or die.

doping Treating a silicon chip with a chemical vapour to make it conduct electricity.

drug A natural or synthetic product that affects the working of the body in some way.

Duralumin An aluminium alloy containing copper, magnesium and manganese. It shows the property of age-hardening, gradually hardening for several days after it has been made.

electrolysis Splitting up a compound in solution or when molten by passing an electric current through it. It is a useful way of producing or refining some metals, including aluminium and copper.

electronics The branch of science concerned with devices that control the flow of electrons, as in computers, TV and radio.

extrusion A method of making plastic rods and pipes by forcing molten plastic through a die.

factory A place in which goods are made, usually with the help of machines.

fermentation A process in which yeast acts upon starch or sugar to produce alcohol and carbon dioxide.

forging Shaping metal by hammering.

Haber synthesis One of the most important processes in the chemical industry, the synthesis of ammonia from its elements – nitrogen and hydrogen. It is named after the German chemist Fritz Haber, who developed it.

heavy chemical A chemical produced in vast quantities, such as sulphuric acid and caustic soda.

herbicide A weedkiller.

hydraulic press A forging machine which exerts a gradual squeezing action on red-hot metal. It works by means of hydraulic (liquid) pressure.

Industrial Revolution The period of history when the widespread introduction of machines led to the creation of industries.

ingot A metal casting made immediately after smelting, of a convenient size for further shaping processes.

injection moulding A method of shaping plastics by squirting molten plastic into a water-cooled mould.

integrated circuit A circuit in which all components and pathways are integrated into the same piece of semiconductor, usually silicon.

interchangeable parts Ones that are almost identical. They hold the key to mass-production.

invar An alloy of iron and nickel with traces of other metals. It is unusual in that it expands or contracts hardly at all when the temperature changes.

lathe The foremost machine tool, on which a machining process called turning is carried out. The workpiece is turned, or rotated, and tools are brought in to remove metal.

machining Shaping metal by means of machine tools, such as lathes, grinding machines and milling machines.

man-made fibres Fibres produced by processing natural materials and also those produced wholly from chemicals.

margarine A butter substitute made these days mainly from plant oils, such as sunflower oil.

mass-production The production of goods on a vast scale, usually by the assembly of interchangeable parts on a production line.

mechanization The introduction of machines, particularly to industry.

microchip An alternative name for a silicon chip, particularly a microprocessor, a chip that can act as a computer by itself.

milling A common machining process in which metal is removed by a rotating toothed cutting wheel.

pasteurization A method of temporarily sterilizing milk and other foods by heating them briefly. It is named after the French chemist who devised it, Louis Pasteur.

petrochemicals Chemicals obtained by processing petroleum in a refinery.

pharmaceuticals Another name for drugs.

pilot plant A small-scale chemical plant, built to assess the performance of a new process.

plastic A synthetic material made up of long molecules which can be moulded into shape by heat.

polymerization A chemical reaction in which a substance with small molecules (the monomer) is converted into a substance with large molecules (the polymer).

printed circuit A circuit made up of a thin layer of copper, which is deposited on a circuit board by a method similar to that used in the production of printing plates.

prototype A full-sized working model of something, made before full-scale production begins.

rayon An artificial fibre produced from the cellulose in cotton fibres or woodpulp.

raw materials Basic materials from which other materials are manufactured.

refining Purifying or converting materials into a more useful form; for example, petroleum and metals.

riveting Joining together pieces of metal by means of headed metal pins.

robot A machine that works automatically under computer-control.

semiconductor A material that conducts electricity slightly when impurities are added to it. Silicon is the most common semiconductor.

silicon chip The name given to a thin wafer of silicon, which carries thousands of electronic circuits, and which can act as part of a computer's circuits, or indeed as a computer itself.

smelting Heating an ore at high temperature in a furnace in order to reduce it to metal.

soldering A method of joining metals by melting solder in between them. It is commonly used for joining copper wires in electronic circuits. Solder is a tin-lead alloy with a low melting point.

spinneret The spinning gland of the silkworm; a device for producing artificial fibres, such as rayon.

spinning Drawing out and twisting short fibres to make continuous yarn, or thread.

steel The most important metal by far. It is an iron alloy, containing traces of carbon and other metals.

sulphuric acid The most important industrial chemical, chemical formula H_2SO_4. It is made by the contact process.

superphosphate A widely used artificial fertilizer made by treating phosphate rock with sulphuric acid.

synthetic fibres Textile fibres made by processing synthetic, plastic materials. Nylon was the original synthetic fibre.

thermoplastic A plastic that softens again when heated.

thermoset Or thermosetting plastic; one that sets hard and rigid when moulded and which does not soften again when heated.

turning A method of machining, carried out on a lathe.

TVP Short for texturized vegetable protein, a meat substitute made from soya beans.

unit operations Standard methods used to process physically chemical materials during manufacture. They include distillation, mixing and filtering.

unit processes Standard chemical reactions carried out during chemical manufacture. They include oxidation, cracking and polymerization.

viscose The common form of rayon, consisting of pure cellulose fibres, which are regenerated from solution.

weaving Interlacing lengthwise (warp) and crosswise (weft) threads to make cloth. It takes place on a machine called a loom.

welding Joining together pieces of metal by means of fusion, or melting touching parts.

woodpulp The raw material for making paper, obtained by breaking down wood into fibres by means of grinding or chemicals.

Index

Page numbers in *italics* rcfcr to pictures.

Further Reading

How Things are Made by Felicity Brooks (Usborne, 1989)
Plastics by Jacqueline Dineen (Young Library, 1986)
Focus on Resources series (Wayland)
Modern Industry by C. A. R. Hills (Batsford, 1988)
How is it Done? (Readers Digest, 1990)
Collins Guide to Modern Technology by Robin Kerrod (Collins, 1983)
Twentieth Century Industry by Rupert Matthews (Wayland, 1989)
Technology in Action series (Wayland)
Textiles by Kathryn Whyman (Gloucester Press, 1988)

Picture Credits